turn me on or off

Solsiree Skarlinsky

TABLE OF CONTENTS

INTRODUCTION:

Among Angela Carter's assortment of essays, novels, and short stories, critics have heralded *The Bloody Chamber* as a collection that is often resistant to patriarchal power while also indulging in both the macabre, and the opulent. Furthermore, the collection itself is often described as a space that, "deliberately defeats the reader's expectations by emancipating women's bodies from attributions of cultural shame, empowering women characters with independence and agency, and bitterly denouncing the arrogant cruelty of human predators" (Henke 48). Despite being touted as a feminist, Carter also received heavy backlash, as she eventually confessed that her short stories were often riddled with too much violence. In 1969, Carter won the Somerset Maugham award, and afterwards, lived in Japan for three years. As an expatriate, she studied Japanese manga and anime, with a focus on the masochism and sadism embedded within the comics (Barker 2). These observations and themes of masochism and sadism eventually threaded into her own fiction, and have roused interest and critique within several feminist communities.

Although Carter received harsh reception by radical feminists such as Andrea Dworkin in her celebration of the Marquis de Sade, Carter's play on fragmentation, in fact, empowers her protagonists. Carter believed that the Marquis de Sade was misogynistic, but she also argued that de Sade congruently revered women as beings of both sexual and political power. Further, Carter's female protagonists struggle against a biological essentialist[1] view, and respond to such treatment by portraying radical

fragmentation by viewing themselves as both subject, and object. Fragmentation resists

an essentialist view, in which oppressive patriarchal characters objectify the fixed essence

that is woman. In contrast, when the protagonist's view themselves as fragmented subject

and object, these women can then objectify themselves. Fragmentation is accomplished

when the protagonist's reverse their roles through a thematic reflective gaze that occurs

within an assortment of mirrors[2] in the novel. Consider that the protagonists view not

only themselves within the mirror, but also view themselves in relation to other objects.

As a body, or an object, that can face her own finitude[3] in relation to others, she is also

subject through her subjective experience in relations to the world[4]. For example, the

protagonist within "The Tiger's Bride" depersonalizes and detaches herself from the

image she sees within the mirror, and as such, views herself as object, while also in

relation to the other objects in that space. As she calls out to her reflection, she states: "all

---

[1] see Susan Henke, *The Female Face of Shame,* these biological essentialist roles that
Carter's protagonist struggle with are the "essentialist role of the anatomical body" or the
notions that there are fixed essences of what it is to be a woman. As such, women are
objectified and subjugated by men according to their biological sex, "dominated by
appetite" and are therefore, "carnally contaminated" (49).

[2] According to Jacques Lacan's study of the mirror phase, infants recognize themselves in
a mirror as fragmented, as there is tension between the subject viewing themselves in the
mirror and the image within it (Kearney 274).

[3] Death

[4] This formation of subject in relation to object will further be unpacked in the chapter
that analyzes Merleau-Ponty.

2

I saw was a pale hollow-eyed girl whom I scarcely recognized" (73). Thus, the protagonist has objectified herself, becoming a fragmented subject and object, and most importantly, as a phenomenological being-in-the-world.

The play on the protagonist as both subject and object within the looking glass is further revealed within the title story "The Bloody Chamber," where the protagonist loses her virginity in a room covered in mirrors that reflect and refract her image. As the protagonist consummates her marriage, she does so under her own gaze. Carter's themes of flesh, and fragmentation, as presented in the mirrors, allow the protagonist to objectify herself, thus making her the subject viewing herself as object[5] (Fabian 3). Furthermore, such an act allows for "radical alienation of the self from any contact with the other" (Johnson, xii). Therefore, one can understand why Angela Carter viewed the works of the Marquis de Sade in such a positive light. The masochism and sadism within de Sade's text becomes a space that portrays women as beings freed from the ties of sex as an act that only equates to procreation, or male pleasure. Instead, sex acts as a space for female pleasure, and in fact, as one where women also wield the power of pain over men, as seen in de Sade's character Juliette[6]. As such, Carter's view of masochism and sadism is of "the most radical attempt in the field of sexual politics to promote the fundamental purpose of sex being simply pleasure" (Sheets 693). In contrast, many take issue with

---

[5] In a similar vein, Jacques Derrida critiques Rousseau's writings on masturbation, wherein the act of masturbation is a symbolic union of both subject and object, and where both could become one.

[6] See Marquis de Sade, *Juliette*

3

these claims, as de Sade also illustrated several instances of rape, and female subjugation, as demonstrated through his character Justine[7].

Carter brings these issues of fragmentation, gender, sex, and patriarchal undoing to light within her work, and although these themes are foregrounded in her writing, causing several critics to focus mainly upon these issues, I contend that there is much more to be unearthed in terms of body and spatial relations. Most importantly, these instances of fragmentation also underscore the division between flesh and the world, and therefore, highlight intimate body and spatial relations. Carter, beneath the veil of fairy tales, allows the reader to confront everyday relations to the world[8]. Her collection, *The Bloody Chamber*, and specifically the short story, "The Lady of the House of Love," allow the notions of fragmentation, gender, sex, and patriarchal undoing to coalesce and engage with the theory of epigenetics, as well as with Merleau-Ponty's *Phenomenology of Perception*. In keeping with this idea, a problematizing of the subject and object dichotomy of body and world, these dichotomies instead collapse and bleed into one another. Thus, this thesis will examine the corporeal haunting of the countess and the epigenetic marks embedded within her flesh, and how it later unravels in tandem with Merleau-Ponty's *Phenomenology of Perception*, where he stated: "Our own body is in the world as the heart is in the organism: it keeps the visible spectacle constantly alive, it breathes life into it and sustains it inwardly" (203). Likewise, the theory of epigenetics

_____

[7] See Marquis de Sade, *Justine, or the Misfortunes of Virtue*

[8] See Martin Heidegger, *Being and Time*

4

considers body and space, as it analyzes the coding of our DNA, and the epigenetic marks that impact phenotypical traits (Weinhold 163).

Phenomenological notions of the relationship between subject and object even arise in the description of Angela Carter's death from cancer at the age of 51. Paul Barker, one of Carter's first editors, said: "She dies untimely, and everyone burst out weeping. The obituaries give her better notice than anything she ever wrote received in her lifetime. Her book sells out within three days of her death. She becomes the most read contemporary author on English university campuses. Her last story, finished during her final illness, sells 80,000 copies in paperback. She has arrived. But she is dead. No magic, and no fame, can alter that" (3). Barker highlights Carter's own absence and presence, as she has both "arrived" and yet is "dead." As an individual who has "arrived" she acts as subject, but as one that is dead, is simultaneously, an object. Philosophers, such as Martin Heidegger, posit this notion of an individual as an object in death. He conjectured that when Dasein (there-being) is no longer in the world, Dasein's corpse still remains within the world as one that is objectively present. Therefore, the body still inhabits this world as a corpse, one that Dasein abandons and casts in the world for others to grieve. One encounters the body as something unliving, therefore as an object that still shows intentionality towards others, and specifically, the body shows intentionality towards the bereaved. These topics will be further covered in Chapter 1.

Further, Angela Carter's work signifies a union of the disciplines of science, literature, and philosophy. In the same vein that Carter has de-alienated object and subject, I propose that her work unifies disciplines that are often quite polarized from one another: natural science, literature, and continental philosophy. Therefore, this text becomes a space of hybridization, where these disciplines melt in a manner not unlike that of the body and its environment. These disciplines are usually viewed as discrete areas rigidly placed within a hierarchy of value. Examples of hierarchal values placed today are the burgeoning schools dedicated to STEM research, with the notable depletion of funding for the arts. Thus, when understood as separate and isolated disciplines, some have hierarchal value over the others. But if one considers science, literature, and continental philosophy under lenses such as deconstruction, the theory of epigenetics, and Merleau-Ponty's phenomenology, these disciplines can be seen in a more global sense rather than as independent and positioned as stand-alone disciplines. Therefore, a hybridization[9] of the disciplines of science, philosophy, and literature does not only merit further investigation, but is already occurring in texts such as "The Lady of the House of Love." Carter's short story illustrates how deconstruction shatters Western metaphysical thought by displacing and deferring the violent nature of hierarchal positioning embedded within disciplinary dichotomies, such as science over philosophy, or the quantitative over qualitative data. Like Carter's protagonists, this thesis aims to view itself within the looking glass. Further, through such fragmentation it seeks to view itself as both subject and object; that is, as a textual object in the world, relating to the world, and blending the aforementioned disciplines.

In order to understand how epigenetics and continental philosophy are often divorced, their positions towards the other will first be explained. For example, Merleau-

---

[9] see shifting frameworks in education from STEM to STEAM at stemtosteam.org

Ponty understood science to be an *ex post facto* abstraction. As such, it is a discipline that deals with ideas that presupposed facts, in comparison to philosophy, which seeks not to presuppose, but rather to anticipate. Therefore, the causal and physiological account of perception emerges after the phenomenon has occurred. Furthermore, Merleau-Ponty chastises the sciences for being "grounded," or in other words, for acting as a discipline that prides itself as an area where a "complete" account of "nature" can be given. In this way, Ponty conjectures that science presumes truths to be stable and fixed. Yet by including phenomena into such logic, reason will serve as "radically intersubjective, a communal text with each scientific mind co-authors with others" (Kearney 78). In comparison, epigenetics has been recounted as a science where "its underlying mechanisms has greatly increased, causing some to describe it in terms of a 'field' rather than just a 'phenomena'" (*Epigenetics* 29). Yet, I conjecture that this theory is not a grounded field, but one that harkens towards the image that Merleau-Ponty invokes. It acts as one that is both constituted by the past, yet open or still to be constituted in the future. As such, the formation of the theory is not only open to meaning, but the phenomenon itself is one derived by "openness." This openness is referenced in the phenomenological term by being-in-the-world, and furthermore, as a body written by the pen that is space. The active enveloping of body and space are indicated through both epigenetic expression, and Merleau-Ponty's philosophy.

The particulars of being-in-the-world in terms of body and space will further be explored throughout this thesis. In order to understand how these threads of philosophy and science interweave within the short story, "The Lady of the House of Love," and how in tandem, they connect and disconnect in light of fragmentation as a "turning on" and "turning off," these theories need to be postulated clearly. Therefore, the first chapter will unpack Merleau-Ponty's *Phenomenology of Perception*, and the second chapter will briefly summarize the theory of epigenetics. The final chapter will become their meeting ground, where points of intersection and divergence in Angela Carter's short story "The Lady of the House of Love" will be analyzed

CHAPTER I: MY BODY AS THE MEDIUM FOR HAVING A WORLD

"Full of merit, yet poetically, man dwells on this earth." –Friedrick Hölderlin

"Amputees suffer pains, cramps, itches in the leg that is no longer there. That is how she felt without him, feeling his presence where he no longer was."
– Gabriel García Márquez, *Love in the Time of Cholera*

Because of the nature of this thesis, which is to view itself in relation to other disciplines and studies, this chapter will unpack several key concepts of Maurice Merleau-Ponty's *Phenomenology of Perception.* It is vital for such concepts to undergo full explication and analysis in a single chapter to articulate properly that the body is at the core of Merleau-Ponty's philosophy, and that there is no phenomenological separation of "I" and the lived body that is open to the world. The lived body is the principle idea that underscores my argument that the body and the world alter one another. These explications allow for an openness to occur within this dialogue, where both reader and writer, in unison, can trace the lines of body and spatial relations that intersect within Carter's short story.

Primarily, this chapter will analyze, and define what Merleau-Ponty meant in terms of the body image, and the body's relations to space. In addition, the relation of body and space will further be elucidated by two major case studies observed by Merleau-Ponty: psychic blindness in a patient named Schneider, and the sensation of the phantom limb. These studies do not only examine how the body enacts within space, but also why one should consider the body a necessary component in the study of our being[10]. In examining Merleau-Ponty's studies and notions, one can unearth their relations to the theory of epigenetics, and how Angela Carter's "The Lady of the House of Love," acts as a necessary bridge between traditionally divorced disciplines of continental philosophy, science, and literature. As aforementioned in the introduction, Merleau-Ponty critiqued the sciences, and championed phenomenology as a needed and necessary conscience for science, where truths cannot be stable and fixed. Yet, despite such critiques, Carter's short story manages to be an emblem of both epigenetics and body/space continental philosophy, and allows for such conversations to not only exist, but to gear one towards the other. One can see intimate connection between body and spatial relations within the science of epigenetics, and in a similar vein, the philosophy of such relations in Merleau-Ponty's work. Contrary to the Cartesian notion of body and space as separate and passive, Merleau-Ponty proposes that space is an extension of body, and that body is an extension of space. Since the body acts within space, it is then aware, and experiences the world according to that presence. Merleau-Ponty posits that "I am not in space and time, nor do I conceive space and time; I belong to them, my body combines with them and includes them" (PP 140). The body, inhabits its environment, and thus, belongs to space and time through a contextualized presence.

Merleau-Ponty's third chapter "The Spatiality of One's Own Body and Motility" in *Phenomenology of Perception* begins with a meditation on our interactions with

---

[10] Merleau-Ponty's work stems from Martin Heidegger's study of phenomenology, as such being can be considered in terms of Heidegger's Dasein, that is as a being indebted to its being. As Dasein, it is our task to question and analyze our own being. Dasein is (da) here or there and neither here nor there, and (sein) as being. (King, 47) Dasein exists to understand being, and therefore, to also understand the possibility that it can also not be.

objects, such as the simple interaction of laying a hand on a table near an ashtray. According to Merleau-Ponty, our hand does not simply rest besides the ashtray, but both are instead "enveloped" within one another (98). Therefore, body and space formsa system as a new relation to Gestalt psychology[11] and summation, which Merleau-Ponty relates to body image. That is, rather than the body being viewed as one composed like a mosaic or a collection of points, the body is viewed as whole or in sum. For example, the body is not simply a collection of parts, like an arm hooked onto a torso, and that beneath these parts there are other parts such as the nerves, veins, and other systems. Instead, the body is a whole with pieces that are just in relation to one another, but most importantly, are interacting in sum. Previously, body image was understood as a collection of moments of awareness, bodily experience, and the sensation of possessing the body. Yet, this definition was problematic because it relied on association, one composed of images where the body acts in relation to these images. For example, viewing the body in terms of images would be like understanding my hand as belonging to an imagined outline of my body. That is to say, when I look at my hand, my perception only affords me the image of my hand, and in order to understand it as a whole (like a point in a collection) I would than imagine the outline of the rest of my body, as I cannot see it. In a way, I first view myself as an outlined whole, and break myself down into parts when I stare down at my arm. Thus, Merleau-Ponty expands the definition of body image as one not confined

---

[11] the whole is greater than the sum of its parts. According to Irvin Rock, and Stephen Palmer of "The Legacy of Gestalt Psychology," parts of a song or film interact with one another in order to form a whole, and therefore the distinct qualities of its parts do not equate the distinctness of the whole. Instead, the whole should be understood as something altogether different, while also being stringent on perception.

11

by images, or a lived-through present experience. Instead, body image should be viewed through that which anticipates our experience, acting as a horizon of possibility[12] that our body anticipates as the space around the body. Thus, the body image is constructed by the spatiality of my positioning, and by my situation, and such, the space I am in informs my body. I am no longer viewing my arm as a point that belongs to an outlined body, but as a total body that is informed by space and time.

The concept of body image being informed by space is further elucidated by Merleau-Ponty's illustration of the body as a comet. If one holds a table, our body trails behind it, and therefore, the position of the hands is stressed upon within our perception. That is not to say that I am unaware of my body, and my hands are the only focal point of my being, but that my body is "swallowed" or understood by the position of my hands on the table. In this sense, my hands become an anchor of the active body that is on or near objects. Therefore, one understands the body in relation to other objects within the world. Thus, "the body image is finally a way of stating that my body is in the world," and as such, is one that exists towards and within the horizon of possibility. As Merleau-Ponty

---

[12] meaning does not blossom from words or within things themselves, but it is housed in the structure of our understanding. Therefore, the world is our horizon of understanding as such, and we move through this horizon. It is a manifold that then extends into the horizon of possibility from these relations. According to King, "the horizon of possibilities formed in and by transcending freedom opens up the distance between how Dasein already is and how he can be." (182) Under the possibility of Dasein's horizon to be, Dasein can also only understand itself by the possibilities that it also cannot be. Being at stake hints towards this not, and it is further unfolded into the "nothing" that is the condition of understanding. If Dasein could only be, it cannot understand itself. Why would one question being if it was always to be? That is why the not is the source of possibility for Dasein, and then it can recognize itself as such, as one that exists, and as one indebted to its being.

posited: "The only solution along this road would be to recognize that the body's spatiality has no meaning of its own to distinguish it from object spatiality," and thus, we garner meaning through a multiplicity of space that lends itself to the universal space (101). Bodily experiences blossom through spaces such as the objective space, and the intelligible space, and are further informed by these spaces through motility. Through movements within these spaces, the body notably inhabits such spaces, and vice-versa.

Merleau-Ponty explains this notion of motility, space, and being through a psychological study done on a patient with "psychic blindness." The patient named Schneider could not perform movements with his eyes closed. Merleau-Ponty terms these movements as abstract since they are not acted within active situations. For clarity, consider abstract movements like a mime's gestured based performance but with eyes closed. Thus, a mime will answer a telephone call without actually holding the phone, or mimic ringing a doorbell lacking the actual objects to perform that task. In contrast, a concrete movement occurs within the actual active situation occurs by manipulating objects with eyes open. Thus, an individual grabbing a phone in order to answer it would be considered a concrete movement. Schneider, on the other hand, could perform these concrete movements but not the abstract. Also, the abstract movements that Schneider was asked to complete were not huge gestures like answering a phone. Instead, the movements that Schneider was asked to perform were minimal, such as bending a finger with eyes closed, and later straightening it. Moreover, the patient could not describe the composition and position of his body, nor point where others were touching his body. Yet, he could grasp objects, and identify touch, and streamlined movements when his eyes were opened. Schneider could achieve an abstract movement by incorporating them slowly, this occurred by practicing abstract movements first concretely. Further, habitual movements were easier for Schneider to perform abstractly, such as removing a handkerchief from his shirt pocket. As such, Schneider could only perform movements in relation to his space, but when his visual access was impaired (by having eyes closed), Schneider's motility within that space was also hindered.

The inabilities to perform abstract movements in patients, such as Schneider, are also lacking a term Merleau-Ponty adopted from Edmund Husserl: an intentional arc. The intentional arc is that which we project to and from--that is, our setting, our past, future, present, and our physical, ideological, and moral situation. As Merleau-Ponty stated, "it is the intentional arc that brings about the unity of the sense, of intelligence, of sensibility, and motility" (136). Therefore, these patients are trapped in the actual, where the body only serves as subject, and as such, they are unable to understand virtual space or other perspective. Therefore, "the body must be attuned to simulations in order to receive them. It must be organized as whole, and actively prepared for the stimulations it encounters, and all of this challenges the abstract image of the body as a fundamentally passive recipient of external forces" (Hass, 80). For this reason, Schneider is able to swat the mosquito stinging him, but cannot point to a portion of his body. Through the lived body, we can perform movements that are abstract even with a lack of concrete purpose, and thus, hinge on anticipation of being-in-the-world, even through virtual spaces like the imagination. The body image, according to Merleau-Ponty, was stringent of the embodied consciousness, so one could not divorce the imagination from perception. As such, the imagination allows us to perform abstract movements like miming, where there

is not actual concrete purpose. Thus, it is through the imagination that abstract
movements can be completed.

Most importantly, in this regard, one must consider one's own thought and how it
links, and extends into the world through a synthesis. That is, subjects must not only be in
the world, but also posit or show, another term from Husserl, intentionality[13] within the
world. Therefore, how the subject accesses the world must be self-evident. An example is
when one points towards the eyes for seeing, or towards the ears for hearing. This shows
that both sensory organs were given as an access point to the world, and their parallel of
sight and sound can be lived and experienced before its actual conception. Therefore, the
world must first exist or as Merleau-Ponty posited, act as a primary meaning, like the
layout of my home, and later garner secondary meaning through my motility within that
space. As such, it is a space where motility can be achieved with eyes closed due to
mental thought and mapping, or a recourse conceptual analysis.

Our primary world sets up a blue print, one that we later enact within by moving
through the secondary world; this is the synthesis of consciousness, but one must also
consider how space and time impact one another. One that brings itself before itself, and

---

[13] For Heidegger, who stemmed from Husserl's study of being, the term existence,
insofar as it is only becoming of being (Dasein), is not extended to all beings. It is
antithetical to the traditional ontology of existence, or an existence that amounts to
presence. Dasein is because it exists. But, beings unlike Dasein (such as a table) are only
objectively present. Contrary to Dasein, beings that are objectively present are
characterized by their outward manifestations and attributes, therefore expressing
whatness. This is the condition for Dasein to understand its being, and thus, Dasein can
never be independent of these objects. For these beings that are objectively present are
accessible to Dasein. This notion of intentionality is why if we "could not discover things
subjectively—if we could not let them touch us, concern us, be relevant to us—we could
not discover them at all."

thus, before several worlds or spaces that engender primary and secondary meaning. The world-structure, as such, is the basis of Merleau-Ponty's argument of the body and consciousness, "for the true subject of thought is the person who achieves the conversion and resumption of action at this very moment, and it is he who breathes his own life into the non-temporal ghost" (Merleau-Ponty 128). Thus, movement is only learned from the body that has incorporated itself into the world, which is within a realm of understanding it, and reaching out towards it like the object that becomes our anchor, or like the aforementioned chair. We inhabit space and time, but both space and time hinges upon perspective. In other words, our access to this synthesis of time and space must be performed in an original sense, as if it has never been performed before. And that is because it has not occured under this new circumstance of space and time. The scope of time and space reflects and extends onto the embodied subject, and vice-versa, through a new lens that is enacted in every moment of my existence. As Richard Kearney postulated in *Modern Movements in European Philosophy,* "the phenomenon of our embodied consciousness is precisely that 'in-between' realm-- l'entrdeux-- which pre-exists the division into subject and object" (75). Thus, consciousness and the world are not separate and passive, but active and overlapped, woven into the fabric of our existence.

Yet, because of space and time weaving into our existence, there are conflicts within perceptions. An example of a conflict or rupture is Merleau-Ponty's study of Schneider, who lacked this dimension or space, or converting the thought or projected movement into actual movement. As such, the conflict was an issue of "neither motility nor thought, and we are brought to the recognition of something between movement as a

16

third person process and through as a representation of movement--something which is an anticipation of, or arrival at, the objective," and thus, "this can be expressed by saying that for the normal person every movement has a background, and that the movement and its background are 'moments of unique sum'" (110). The background sustains, and follows through like an inspirational beacon that relates and dilates towards subject, and object[14] in attuned perceptions. We are both object and subject. As objects, we react to the world by exterior influences like any other object may, and are governed by scientific principles and law, but also act as subjects in our responses with needs and desires which act upon the world. Further, it is through my subjectivity that I respond to the world, and garner knowledge from the world through the body that acts as the vehicle of my experience that extends into the world. Therefore, the body is not just an object, but also subject, as it is "as true to say that my body is me as that I am my body" (Mathews, 51).

When we consider our body as both subject, and object, it is important to consider how the body acts as a vehicle of time, and space. As individuals, we rarely go about measuring out time an embodied sense, or through our bodies. Instead, we measure time outside of our bodies, through events that occur in our lives. Yet, every once in a while,

---

[14] Ontic existentiell: (ontic) physical, real. This term characterizes beings, and not their being. We must return to the ontic understanding of 'world," and of being since Dasein is understood as being that exists. Ontic and exist are terms that are synonymous, thus existentiell is paralleled to ontic. Heidegger uses ontic existentiell to characterize Dasein's understanding of the concrete. The degree of Dasein's understanding of being, for example if it were only understood in terms of the ontic, does not equate a lesser form of Dasein. Much like Dasein's lostness to the world is still a form of being (echoing the prior note on falleness). King charts the existential schema, and I found that it best elucidated Heidegger's use the following terminology:
"Existentiell is parallel to ontic
Existential (adj) is parallel to ontological
Existential (n) is parallel to category" (46)

we are reminded that our bodies are also keepers of time. Lawrence Hass of *Merleau-*

Ponty's Philosophy elucidates how we are thrown back into our bodies to measure time.

For instance, as individuals with goals and aspirations, we usually view the past as

something that has led us to who we are today, and mark periods of time by what we

would like to gain in a certain stage of life, such as graduating with my degree by the age

of twenty-four. Yet, as Hass indicates, something as simple as the flu can throw one back

to measuring time corporeally, and thus, we measure time through the body altered by the

flu, and are marked by the stages of progression and recovery from the illness. I measure

my time by my sleep, and how my health has progressed as a "weaving back, forth and

through the demands of my organism and the integrative horizons of intentional life," in

terms of what the flesh houses.[15] (88) The flesh, or our body, then houses time and the

---

[15] The veil of the flesh is key in understanding how we, as beings, inhabit and relate with
the world. Notable examples of the role of the flesh are found in both literature, and
materiality. The first is an example most memorable to me, from John Keats' letter to
George and Georgiana Keats on April 21st of 1819. He stated the following in regards to
the vale of soul-making: "Do you not see how necessary a World of Pain and troubles is
to school an Intelligence and make it a soul? A Place where the heart must feel and make
it a soul? A Place where the heart must feel and suffer in a thousand diverse ways!" (358)
Keat's takes to task how suffering and pain has an intrinsic role in our being. Like
Heidegger's anxiety as a mood of pre-understanding, the flesh is then key into our
understanding of being-in-the-world. It is through flesh that, as Merleau-Ponty stated, and
I later highlight, that our ontic relations to the world bursts through. In terms of
materiality, one can consider the role that vellum or parchment had since it derives from
the flesh of an animal such as calfskin, and is manufactured by a long process of flaying,
stretching, soaking, drying, and scraping done by hand. When you touch, and parse
through such manuscripts, you can feel the roughness of the parchment, and the tiny
spindles of hair left from the animal. Manuscripts could be reconstituted since simply
scraping the first layer of skin with a pumice stone could erase the words. The individuals
during the middle ages had an intimate relation with this text, as its materiality was
literally one made of flesh, where readers would interact with the text/body with every
sense—from smell to touch. The role of materiality as an object in our world will further
be teased out in Chapter 3, where this thesis will consider the materiality of Angela
Carter's text as a weaving within our world, and within our being.

world, and one must be mindful of this. How our body is our own timekeeper will be further explicated at the end of the chapter in terms of being-towards-death. Yet, how body and space are actively overlapping needs to be further explained by case studies such as the phantom limb.

The overlap of space and time elucidates Merleau-Ponty's claims that body and space are not divided as we traditionally conceived, and this notion is more explicit in his research of the phantom limb experienced by amputees. The phenomenon of the phantom limb is often understood physiologically, as such one would understand the this sensation of the phantom limb is ascribed to a nerve path that still signals to the brain that the arm is there, when in fact, it is not. The mind and the nervous system are then at the center of the experience, but Merleau-Ponty critiques such an objectivist and physiological framework and believes that further explanation is necessary--even more so in the case of some patients that not only sense that the limb is still there but that it had doubled in size. The limb is described as gigantic until the patient slowly acclimates to accepting that the limb is, indeed, gone. Once this occurs, then the limb size the patient had previously sensed begins to shrink (Matthews, 55). The experience of the phantom limb reveals itself as not the absence of proper and normal functionality of that body part, but as one that "vividly changes one's access to the world" (Morris 113). In other words, when a patient experiences a phantom limb such as a hand, the pieces of the world that would beckon action from the hand—the door bell which calls to be pressed—will continue to signify action in correlation with the hands capacity (even if the hand is no longer there).

Most importantly, although this phenomenon occurs based off perception, it can be changed because this perception springs from conflicted division. The only way to lose the signification that the limb is still there, and in order to alter this experience, a patient must restructure the world so objects correlated with the hand does not call "to be pressed" or "to be strung." Such ruptures of body image like anosognosia and the phantom limb occur due to the rupture of the personal projection (individual), and biological life. Conflicts occur in terms of several divisions, such as: the habit body and the personal body, the impersonal and the personal, the biological and the individual, the sediment and the spontaneous, and finally the organic and the existential. When one fails to perceive, either through actual perceived presence as felt by those that suffer from phantom limb or actual perceived absence as felt by those suffering anosognosia, both are trapped by the objective world[16] and continue to not only allow these perceptions to exist, but to rely on them. The most prominent and relatable example that Merleau-Ponty gives is how one feels after a friend has departed. For example, if a friend has passed and is no longer "before my eyes," one cannot truly feel that loss of this friend until one has allowed for it, and restructured their world according to the loss. In other words, I continue to exist in the world as if my friend was still alive, and similarly, this is what occurs to those suffering a phantom limb. One must restructure so that the personal projection matches the biological life, rather than live a conflicted experience where the world continues to "call" to me within these ruptures.

Since I have covered the habit body and the personal body as noted in the case by Schneider, and the biological and the individual as noted in the case of the phantom limb, I would like to examine the other possible ruptures such as the sedimented and the

---

[16] As seen in Schneider

spontaneous. By examining these ruptures, Merleau-Ponty interrogates the body subject, and suggests that it is integral in being-in-the-world[17]. Merleau-Ponty describes sediments as the "world of thought" or what is left from our mental processes that we then transform into something meaningful through our lived experiences. That which is sedimented is already part of our habits, yet remains open toward possibility to acquire new behaviors (the spontaneous) and form habits through rearranging and renewing the sediments. As precisely noted, such experience will always be new in our being in the world because of time and space (130). Ruptures such as the sedimented and spontaneous, and the habit and personal, create repressions, as seen in the repression of a patient with anosognosia. The repressions allow space for an individual to further understand their emotions, acting like pre-understandings[18] of being-in-the-world. Emotions can overwhelm an individual as they rise within the cracks of the personal and the intentional (like when one has the flu and is thrown back into the body). We must face them through body consciousness. When one is body conscious, we are caught

---

[17] Being-in-the-world rejects the physical concepts of the world, the ontic natural universe, and that things of nature constitute all being. As such, being-in-the-world is not a concept of factual existence, totality, or essence. Dasein's own disclosure of its own being as being underscores being-in-the-world. (King, 52) Heidegger's 'world' is an existential-ontological concept that is understood in the way in which Dasein exists. Further, our understanding of the 'world' stems from the ontic springboard of understanding, and finally, the word 'world' is always in quotes in *Being and Time* because it is a fluid concept, where its meaning reflects the context in which world is understood.

[18] According to Heidegger, this is based on ontological moods such as anguish. Anguish expresses the upmost possibility for being-in-the-world: not being. These moods as pre-understanding allow Dasein a reflective self-awareness to such a degree that Dasein reflects on projected possibilities before Dasein understands them as such. (Kearney, 24)

within a paradox of not being able to face a situation, and are emotionally stunted by it, yet we do not want to escape it. For example, if an accident were to occur, although I do not want to face the tragedy in my life, I also do not want to escape it because this dread is a necessary component in my ontic relations to the world. In this paradox, one lives ecstatically[19]. That is, memories "reopen time lost to us," and thus, we cannot personalize such emotions and traumas such as the phantom limb, or the loss of a loved one (Meleau-Ponty 86). We can only repress, and reconstruct, all which "presuppose the erasure of reality" that such ruptures exist (86).

I would like to close by highlighting being and death. Although *Phenomenology of Perception* did not significantly address this topic, Merleau-Ponty's work is indebted to Heideggerian phenomenology. As such, it would be appropriate to unpack some of the notions of being towards death, and its relations to body in order to examine both epigenetics and the countess' death in Carter's "The Lady of the House of Love." Insofar as man/woman's existence as Dasein is a projection toward the future, the ultimate inevitable end is death. As beings contingent on time, death must represent the end of all possibilities. As Richard Kearney deduced, "All our existence is haunted at every moment by an awareness, which we usually conceal from ourselves, of our own ultimate

---

[19] Dasein is always ahead of itself, and brings all possibility towards itself. But, always returns to the conditions of here, or thrown into the world. Dasein can be, as such, in the gulf of the conditions that he is already limited by. (King, 36) Conditions such as cultural, social, psychological, and so on, but these conditions are not predeterminations (and if these conditions act as such, they work as measures of distance dictated by "they"). Dasein must understand itself in terms of this facticity, to reinterpret, and make meaning by disclosing itself as a possibility.

nothingness—our being-towards-death" (35). The experience of one's death is not one left for the dead to suffer and grieve, but for those who are left behind. I can only experience the death of others. Since death is the end of the experience, how can I experience it? Dasein's death is one only intended for him, and one cannot die for another, because it is one's ownmost death. There can be no substitution, as elucidated by Heidegger: "No one can take the other's dying away from him" (231). Suppose that Dasein did die for another, the other is not relieved from death, it will occur as Dasein's death is always his own. My death is mine, and death is the only end of only my existence.

Given that Dasein's existence must come to end, we are forced to interrogate the meaning of the end. Is it abrupt, or a fading from existence? When we have reached the ultimate possibility (death) and become 'whole' do we reach it in increments, or is it a sudden filling of the possibility we lacked? Heidegger lays out the examples of the shadow of the moon, and an unripe fruit inching towards ripeness to characterize what it means for Dasein to be not-yet whole. Death for Dasein is not an experience of vanishing like rain, or stopping like a road, and it does not necessarily mean fulfilling oneself. The idea of fulfillment is what makes the question of Dasein's end so exigent, because it allows us to understand Dasein's mode of death. For Dasein to be fulfilled, we understand it as reaching a finish line, which is only possible for beings objectively present (like a chair fulfills its purpose until its end). All these modes of disappearing, or finishing characterize the objective presence. A fruit that is objectively present slowly rots away. But as Dasein is born then Dasein is old enough to die, and there is no inching

23

towards an end, it can just be. In that light we understand that if Dasein "can be whole at all, he can be so only from his end" (King, 149).

In conclusion, this chapter has elucidated that we are a body of habit that extends into the world, and as such, we inhabit space and time and "habit expresses our power of dilating our being in the world" (PP 143). It is through our movements that we inhabit space, so as "being in the world" we are being in body. Temporality is also the key to movement, so the meaning of being is also gendered by time through the motility of body, or Merleau-Ponty's "lived-through movement." He stated:

> "How the body inhabits space (and time, for that matter) can be see
> more clearly by considering the body motion because movement is not
> content with passively undergoing space and time, it actively assumes
> them, it takes them up in their original signification that is effaced in
> the banality of established situations." (PP 105)

As such, with this vision of the body and the environment actively inhabiting one another, the following chapter will revisit this idea, but in light of the science of epigenetics. As you read the next chapter, keep Merleau-Ponty's enveloping of the body and space, and how one can alter the other in mind.

CHAPTER II: A GENETIC HAUNTING

"To see what everyone else has seen but to think what nobody else has thought."
–Albert Szent-Gyorgyi

"Asi te amo porque no sé amar de otra manera, sino asi de este modo en que no soy ni eres, tan cerca que tu mano sobre mi pecho es mía, tan cerca que se cierran tus ojos con mi sueño." –Pablo Neruda, Soneto XVII

The theory of epigenetics analyzes the coding of our DNA, and the epigenetic marks that either condense or decondense chromatin to either turn on or turn off a specific gene. Most of the theories that I will be explaining are indebted to my father, Thomas Skarlinsky, who studies genetics in insects and is, in fact, completing a thesis on the genetic makeup of thrips. Alongside our conversations, two key texts were used in this chapter: *The Epigenetics Revolution* by Nessa Carey and *The Developing Genome: An Introduction to Behavioral Epigenetics* by David S. Moore. Epigenetics means "changes in genetic sequences," most notably found in chromatin modifications, a process that threads into both Angela Carter's short story, which we will later observe, and Merleau-Ponty's philosophy (Weinhold 2).

Deoxyribonucleic acid or DNA is wrapped around chromatin, which acts as an instructional guide for the cell. Epigenetic marks lie on the surface of the chromatin as small chemical tags that can either condense, thus obscuring the genetic instructions, or uncoil, and becoming accessible for the cell to read, ultimately influencing gene expression. The process usually occurs during embryonic development, but can also be influenced by the environment outside of the developing embryo. Influences, such as these, occur through a slew of environmental factors such as the mother's diet, and whether she smoked or what her levels of stress were. Most importantly, these epigenetic changes can be transmitted to multiple generations. My first example is a study done by Michael Skinner from Washington State University, where pregnant rats were exposed to an insecticide and fungicide, and their pups were later found to have low level of sperm production or were completely infertile (Weinhold 163). The second study, reviewed by Courtney Griffin, an assistant member in cardiovascular biology research program at the Oklahoma Medical Research Foundation, was conducted in Sweden and England, and traced the impact that diet and smoking in young boys had on their future generations. The long-term study found that "boy who overate or started smoking during their pre-pubescent years, when their sperm was starting to develop, went on to have sons and grandsons with significantly shorter life spans" (Weinhold 160). With this in mind, the notion of epigenetics is one that haunts our own flesh, as we are literally embedded with a community of our ancestors, haunting us with their life choices.

In order to understand these concepts, such as chromatin[20] and how such gene expressions could even occur, I will first review the cell beginning with the DNA, and how it should be examined like a script. For example, when we have a play such as Shakespeare's *The Tempest*, it was created with the intention for it to be performed and thus, only acts as a guide for a multiplicity of others to interpret and enact. A producer can adapt the play to a different setting, and assign character lines or functions to another. For example, Julie Taymor's film adaptation of *The Tempest* converts the main protagonist Prospero into Prospera. Such a small change drastically impacts the plot, and fortunately in Taymor's film, does so for the better. Therefore, we must understand that a

---

[20] According to Carey, chromatin is "DNA in combination with it associated proteins, especially histone proteins" (325).

good script can yield a bad play because variables are not contingent on the script, but on the setting. In terms of genetics, one is simply reading the genetic code, where the entire world, including our own DNA, is in fact, a stage. We have roughly about 50 to 70 trillion cells within our body (Carey 12). All these cells are indebted to our first cell, the zygote, which was created through fertilization. The zygote, or the single diploid cell, is responsible for all the copies that makes up all our body tissues. The zygote undergoes division, thus creating two sister cells that are identical in both physical and genetic makeup, and these cells will also undergo division, until we become the leviathan mass of trillion of cells that we are today. This brings two questions to light: If our cells are exact replicas of the other, how can cells have different roles? And how is our genetic makeup transcribed from one cell to the other?

A scientist named John Gurdon who implanted a nucleus from the cell of an adult toad into an unfertilized egg put this theory to task (Moore 44). The unfertilized egg lacked its own nucleus because the egg underwent ultraviolet light treatments. After the experiment, Gurdon found that the nucleus would start anew and create an entirely new animal when placed in the proper setting. The gene whose script once said: "I am a mature frog" would simply turn off when placed within the jelly-like unfertilized egg sac. When the gene read as "off," the nucleus read the genetic coding as if it said, "I am a newly hatched frog," and therefore began the maturing and developing process once again. The restarting of an older nucleus within a new environment is an example of nuclear transplantation, and how circumstances can influence genetic expression. As Carey stated: "Epigenetics is the 'something' in these cells. The epigenetic system controls how the genes in DNA are used, in some cases, for hundred of cell division cycles, and the effects are inherited when cells divide. Epigenetic modifications to the essential blueprint exist over and above the genetic code, on top of it, and program cells for decades" (18). In the same vein, these codes can also be turned off, and reveal the DNA that was always there. Whether the gene turns on or off can be affected by different factors that I will later review.

But how is DNA replicated? Deoxyribonucleic acid is a molecule that acts like language because it is in fact a code. The DNA is made of a double stranded molecule (or double helix) that is comprised of nucleotide bases that consist of adenine, cytosine, guanine, or thymine. That is, the nucleotide bases are made of adenine, cytosine, guanine, or thymine. The helix is created through a base pairing principle, thus adenine (A) will always pair with thymine (T), and guanine (G) will always pair with cytosine (C). The base pairing principle is key in understanding how the nucleotide base pairs will align to form the double helix, where each strand faces the other following the base-pairing phenomenon. In other words, where guanine faces cytosine, and adenine faces thymine and therefore, creates the double helix (Moore 29).

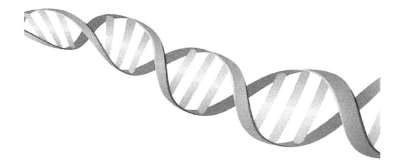

Figure 1. The DNA double helix (*The Atlantic*/John Schwegel)

During the copying process, with the base pairing principle in mind, a perfect

DNA copy in each daughter cell can be achieved. Each cell has six billion base pairs;

therefore, if adenine (A) will always be paired with thymine (T), the chances of error are

lessened drastically in the copying process. Furthermore, the DNA is not copied within

the nucleus but within the cytoplasm of the cell. Triplet nucleotide bases of DNA

correspond to an amino acid, which is in fact a protein base. Therefore, the triplet

nucleotide bases of cytosine (C), adenine (A), and guanine (G) corresponds to the amino

acid glutamine, or thymine (T), adenine (A), and thymine (T) will correspond to the

amino acid tyrosine (Moore 30). These protein bases are given their shape by the amino

acids, which only match according to gene sequence triplets. Therefore, the protein

shapes are ultimately influenced by the DNA sequence. In order for these proteins to be

created and for information from the DNA to be read within the cytoplasm, the

information must be copied to another similar molecule called the RNA. Ribonucleic acid is made of bases like DNA, and undergoes phases of transcription, and translation in order to properly copy the DNA transcript to the daughter cells. How RNA carries information echoes the idea that DNA works like a play or transcript, therefore transcription occurs when there is a successful succession of DNA to RNA, and translation occurs when the transcript (or the DNA sequence) is read, and when protein is finally produced in the cytoplasm. According to Moore, "because protein shapes are what makes them distinctive, it is the order of amino acids in protein--and hence, the order of bases in the responding gene--that make a protein like serotonin function as a neurotransmitter in a brain and a protein like hemoglobin function as an oxygen transporter in blood" (30). Yet, a little less than 2% of our DNA is responsible for creating protein, the other 98 percent is considered non-coding DNA, and recently, scientist have begun to understand the function of it, and have discovered that is intimately connected to epigenetics and gene expression (Carey 53). For example, in *Escherichia coli* bacteria, noncoding DNA can increase or lessen the production of proteins that can digest lactose according to the environment the bacterium is in. Thus, within the *Escherichia coli* cell, if there is a presence of lactose, the bacteria will yield a protein to digest lactose (Carey 56). Therefore, this serves as an example of how environment impacts such expressions, but most importantly, how it does so through noncoding DNA.

Thus, now that the structure and function of the cell, DNA, and RNA have all been explained, epigenetics, and how such expressions can be turned on or off will be reviewed. During the transcription phase, molecules bind to locations on DNA regulatory sites that are made of nucleotide bases. These molecules are called transcription factors. At these points, the genes begin to transcribe while also being regulated. The regulatory sites and the gene that are being regulated are not necessarily next to one another, like a lock and key, but in contrast, can be at quite a distance from the other. The potential distance marks how epigenetic factors affect gene expression by "altering the ability of transcription factors to bind the regulatory sites that regulate the gene activity" (Moore 67). There are three types of epigenetic gene expression that I would like to highlight: DNA methylation, histone methylation, and histone acetylation. DNA methylation occurs simply by adding methyl group to the DNA, which is an epigenetic modification that does not alter, but adds to the DNA sequence, which can affect gene expression by turning a gene "off." Histones are proteins intimately associated with DNA that are ball-like and together form a histone octamer that acts like packing peanuts to hold DNA together (Carey 65). That way the long DNA strands do not just flop around freely within the cell because DNA has a negative charge, and histones have a positive charge, and thus they attract and hold each other together.

Figure. 2 Histones (The University of North Carolina of Chapel Hill/ Brooke Sauer)

Both histone methylation and acetylation are forms of histone modification that cannot only silence a gene expression or "turn off" that expression, but also activate it or

31

"turn on" the expression through histone acetylation where acetyl groups are added to the histone in the same vein as methyl is added to the histone in histone methylation (Carey 65). It is important to note that DNA methylation can be sustained throughout an individual's life, whereas histone modifications such as methylation or acetylation are much more volatile and dynamic (Moore 67). Most importantly, whether the epigenetic marks turn on depends on several factors such as: which chemical group and which histone group is being modified, and which amino acid that bind these group is, in fact, being bound and how many are undergoing the bind. Nessa Carey illustrates how difficult it is to pinpoint the countless combinations of histone modifications, and the intricacy of predicting such combinations. She does so in the most relative way by comparing a chromosome to a Christmas tree. She states:

> Imagine a chromosome as the trunk of a very big Christmas tree. The branches sticking out all over the tree are the histone tails and these can be decorated with epigenetic modification. We pick up the purple baubles, and we put one, two or three purple baubles on some of the branches. We also have green icicle decorations and we can put either one or two of these on some branches, some of which already have purple baubles on them. Then we pick up the red stars but are told we can't put these on a branch if the adjacent branch has any purple baubles. The gold snowflakes and green icicles can't be present on the same branch. And so it goes on, with increasingly complex rules and patterns. Eventually, we've used all our decorations and we wind the lights around the tree. The bulbs represent individual genes. By a magical piece of software programming, the brightness of each bulb is determined by the precise conformation of the decoration surrounding it. The likelihood is that we would really struggle to predict the brightness of most of the bulbs because the pattern of Christmas decoration is so complicated. (68)

I relate the study of genetics to language or coding like Carey's analogy, as it not only takes to task the mathematical prediction of countless combined outcomes, but what these outcomes signify or transcribe. Thus, the language buried within our chromosomes begs to be explored. As such, case studies that highlight the impact and influence that genes hold, and how such modifications not only alter us on a chemical and biological level, but also physiological will be examined.

The first examples will highlight epigenetic changes in nonhumans, beginning with plants and honeybees. It has been observed that epigenetic marks can influence the physical structure within plants and animals. In 1999, scientists photographed the toadflax flower in the United Kingdom (Moore 57). Within the scope of images, the scientist found a flower, the peloric mutant toadflax flower, which seemed to physically belong to a different species of plant. Yet, the flower was of the same species, and the physical differences were due to an epigenetic mark that had silenced, or turned off, the gene expression that would have lead to a normal development (Moore 58). Yet, according to Moore, we cannot simply equate that an epigenetic mark, such as the one aforementioned, directly caused a trait. Instead, such a trait should be accounted for in light of the mark, and it should be observed by that gene expression that is either turned on or turned off (58). A notable example is in a honeybee colony. All the females of a colony are genetically identical in birth, and the only environmental difference between queens and worker bees were their diets. Therefore, there is a correlation between the bee's diets, their genetic expression and their different behavioral and physiological development. Queen bees consume a diet of only royal jelly for the rest of their lives, while worker bees only consume royal jelly during the larvae stage (Carey 280). Royal jelly is a milky nutritious substance that secretes from the head of worker bees. It seems that "a protein in royal jelly increases concentrations of a hormone in female larvae, which contributes to the differentiation into queens" and thus, queen bees develop mature ovaries to reproduce, whereas worker bees are sterile, and as such, are not only unable to reproduce, but also have shorter life-spans (Carey 281). Genes do not equal our characteristics, but work in collaboration with epigenetics, environmental, and other non-genetic factors, and thus, we must consider how dietary and environmental changes influence our own genetic expression.

Next, I would like to move to different studies done on twins to confirm the impact genetic expression can have, particularly in twins that usually are regarded as "identical." For example, if one twin is diagnosed with schizophrenia, the other's risk increases to 50% compared to the .05% risk of the rest of the population (Carey 12). We need to consider that if the genetic code is the same for both twins, why is the risk not one hundred percent, rather than just half? One needs to consider early childhood exposure, and environmental factors, as the environment "speaks" to us and alters our access to it. For example, in the Spanish National Cancer Centre in Madrid, Spain, forty pairs of twins were studied (Moore 57). Identical twins, unlike single individuals whom stem from a zygote, are monozygotic. Therefore, they both shared a single zygote. In the studies, it was found that these monozygotic identical twins had the same genetic expression, but as they aged, their experiences, and different lifestyles resulted in divergent DNA and histone acetylation. The different experiences that each twin had left "marks" on their gene expression. According to Moore, other similar studies held different conclusion, such as twins born with different genetic expression that in theory reflected "prenatal environments" that differed in one way or another for each (57).

34

Another example that I would like to highlight from Carey is the Dutch Hunger Winter. In 1944, a famine occurred during the last winter of World War II during a Nazi food blockade in the Netherlands. As a result, "twenty-two thousand people died and the desperate population ate anything they could find, from tulip bulbs to animal blood" (Carey 91). The survivors of the famine had all undergone severe malnutrition at the same time, and as such, became subjects of speculation on the impact diet and the environment could have on future generations. Particularly, pregnant women were observed, and it was concluded that if a mother was malnourished during the last few months of pregnancy, but well fed during the first, the baby would be born small. In contrast, if the mothers were malnourished during the beginning months, but well fed later in her term, the baby would be born with an average weight (Carey 91). Afterwards, the infants were observed into adulthood, and the findings were recorded which matched several studies done on similar famines, such as the Great Chinese Famine. The smaller babies did not only have higher obesity rates than the rest of the population, but were also at higher risk of developing mental disorders such as schizophrenia, and abnormal neurological systems such as spinal bifida, and cerebral palsy (Moore 183).

Furthermore, another case study concerns human diseases and genomic imprinting disorders, such as Prader-Willi Syndrome[21] and Angelman Syndrome[22]. Both

---

[21] Prader-Willi Syndrome is a genetic disorder characterized by a short stature, low muscle tone, behavioral issues and an unquenchable hunger, usually resulting in the individual to be overweight or obese.

disorders are caused by the same loss of information in the genotype within chromosome 15 called the 15q11-q13 area of the chromosome (*Epigenetics* 441). Yet, despite both disorders sharing the same genotype, they have completely different phenotypes. The different phenotypes are associated with the sex of the parents in which these traits were inherited from. Therefore, if the area that was lost derives from the mother, the individual would have a different phenotype resulting in Angelman Syndrome. In contrast, although this individual would express the same genotype, if it derived from the father, the individual would have Prader-Willi Syndrome. The lost area of information, or 15q11-q13, in chromosome 15 is an example of genetic mutation. Yet, through DNA methylation, the paternal or maternal chromosome is silenced indicating an epigenetic cause for these disorders (Carey 139). For example, if an individual inherited two normal copies of chromosome 15 from their mother, or uniparentaldisony, the individual would have Angelman Syndrome because the father's chromosome was silenced because of epigenetic expression through DNA methylation (*Epigenetics* 443). In contrast, if both copies were from the father because the mother's chromosome was silenced, the individual would have Prader-Willi Syndrome. The Angelman Syndrome and Prader-Willi Syndrome case is a key and fascinating study in understanding epigenetics and familial imprinting, showing that despite having identical "coding" an individual could have two radically different disorders.

Lars Byrgen conducted the final case I would like to examine. The study was led

---

[22] Angelman syndrome is also a genetic disorder but characterized by the nervous system, and as such the individual has delayed mental and physical development while maintain a happy and childlike demeanor.

in a small rural town in northern Sweden named Överkalix. The town itself has kept detailed records of the crop yields that it has produced, and good records of those that lived within the town since 1799 (Moore 180). Through this set of data, Byrgen was able to analyze the manifold of cross-generational epigenetic impact that famine had bestowed upon each family. For example, harvests also reflected whether certain members of the community were either well fed or malnourished. Due to these correlations, Byrgen and his colleagues examined 239 individuals from either 1890, 1905, or 1920, and if future generations of these crop failures were impacted. According to Moore, the researchers found that there was a direct impact between environment, ancestor's experiences, and inheritance through epigenetic expression. They found that "insufficient food was available when a particular male was in his slow growth period, his future son was less likely to die from complications of cardiovascular disease," and surprisingly, even within his future grandchild (181). On the other hand, men who had an excess amount of food during their slow growth period were fourfold more likely to die from diabetes-related issues. The rates included the individual's third generation, or grandchildren. The increased mortality rate occurred in grandchildren who did not eat in abundance during their slow growth rate, instead they paid for the sins of their father, and as such, found that it occurred through a "reprogramming of methylation imprints" (Moore 181). Now, if a grandmother experienced hunger during her slow growth period, her granddaughter's lived longer, but in contrast, if the grandmother ate abundantly during the slow growth period, her granddaughter had twice the risk of dying at any age, for any reason than a control group of female lifespans.

Overall, these relations force one to consider our diets and our environment, as they can profoundly influence not only ourselves but our future generations. As such, experiences influence our gene expression, and this fact cannot be dismissed. Geneticist are exploring the power that epigenetics can wield, because if an expression can be turned on like a light that showcases the terrors of shorter life-spans or disorders conjured by our phenotype, perhaps one can also turn it off, and revel in things of beauty. Such a light switch, and our extension of being into the world, can be observed both within the disciplines of science and philosophy, but are elucidated in Carter's "The Lady of the House of Love" which will be examined in the following chapter.

CHAPTER III: THE SYMPTOM OF HER DISORDER

The previous chapters elucidate how Merleau-Ponty and the theory of epigenetics gear towards one another, and already are very much in conversation. I argue that such a conversation is further evident in literary platforms, explicitly Angela Carter's short story "The Lady of the House of Love," where several instances throughout the narrative hint toward a union between body and spatial relations and epigenetic marks within the countess. For example, there is the presence of the countess' vampire ancestors looming within the shadows. As the narrator states, these ghosts haunt "even at midday, shadows that have no source in anything visible," in crevices within the countess' home as she walks "under the eyes of the portraits of her demented and atrocious ancestors, each one of whom, through her, projects a baleful posthumous existence" (Carter 107). The embodied projection of her ancestor already traces to the environment, where these shadows exist and prosper. Insofar that the environment is comprised of these ancestral shadows, the countess is also consumed by them. In summary, "The Lady of the House of Love" reimagines the Countess Nosferatu as a vampire queen trapped by her ancestors who manifest themselves throughout the city in Romania, and through the cold dead flesh of the protagonist. She is fitted into her mother's bridal gown and casts her own unwavering tarot, which constantly reads the same outcome: wisdom, death, and dissolution. She is an effulgent beauty that echoes the "symptom of her disorder," as she must survive by consuming the blood of shepherd and gypsy boys, as fluids coalesce and drip down her pale cheeks. And she does so in contempt and disgust of her own diet, one composed of blood and tears. Her cards finally change when a virginal British officer arrives on her dilapidated doorstep, and casts the constellations of love and death within her tarot. As such, she spares the life of the officer, and through this choice, she faces her own finitude and dies. Under the guise of a vampire fairy tale in "The Lady of the House of Love," Carter enables the reader to confront realms of materiality, the sciences, and being-in-the-world. Therefore, this chapter will analyze how these threads tie, and how they unravel. The chapter will trace the ebb and flow of materiality, epigenetics, and body and spatial relations within the text.

Carter was a medievalist at the University of Bristol, where she concentrated in Chaucer studies, and favored Spenserian allegories. Thus, it is not overreaching to assume that Angela Carter was aware of the importance of the material object since the study of medieval manuscripts encompasses the object itself, and the sensations that the material object affords its readers. The study of the materiality of a text explores notions of the text as body, and as aforementioned, how one interacts intimately with a text. The material object weighed much more heavily during the Middle Ages because the codex comprised of vellum, therefore interactions with a text were ones where skin interacted with skin. Critics, such as Michael Camille, touted manuscripts and material texts as visual noise. In regards to manuscripts, one would be swathed by sensory experiences, beginning with the smell of parchment to the illuminated visual images embedded throughout, and where words are digested. Such interactions bled into erotic associations as medieval readers would kiss devout texts, and book making was considered a reproductive sacrilege, echoing notions that writers such as John Milton surmised in *Areopagitica*: "For books are not absolutely dead things, but do contain a potency of life in them to be as active as that soul was whose progeny they are; nay, they do preserve as in a vial the purest efficacy and extraction of that living intellect that bred them" (113).

Texts even become progenies of readers since they would leave their bodily imprints on texts as readers interacted with them. For example, medieval readers would impart extractions of themselves upon the text since vellum was easily edited by simply buffing a word away with a pumice stone, and thereafter, used again as if it were new. Thus, readers would directly edit mistakes or add to the text with ease.

If one considers this notion of extraction and imprinting, do modern readers engage in the same manner when they interact with a text? Furthermore, in the hands of the reader, is the physical text not also altered and made anew? For instance, if one considers the death of the author, meaning making already lands within the hands of the reader. That is to say, if readers can alter a text in terms of the distinct meaning that is achieved, than readers can also alter texts on a physical level. Therefore, I posit the text acts as a material performance of my argument on two levels: (1) If one views the text as dead matter within our world, through its intentionality, it then consumes us like Merleau-Ponty's philosophy posits, and (2) The markings that one adds to the material body of the text alters our access to it, and therefore, alters its expression like epigenetic marks alter gene expression.

Therefore, in contrast to Milton's books that contain life, if one considers books as dead matter, then such matter shows intentionality through our interactions with it. That is, such objects are constituents of our being. Likewise, these interactions harken towards Merleau-Ponty *Phenomenology of Perception*, because if one considers the physical text as world, specifically through the act of reading and writing as interactions with this world, are we not consumed by it? Do we not dilate into this world, and in the same token, become marked by it? As such, this further exemplifies Merleau-Ponty's philosophy where the body combines and includes space and time, where the other envelops one. For example, the physical material text of Angela Carter's collection *The Bloody Chamber* that I own is an object that acts within the world through meaningful relations to other objects. That is, I view the collection, in relations to the desk it is on, in relation to the computer laying next to it, in relation to the stack of papers to the right of the computer, in relation to the room, and etc. Therefore, the novel, in relations to all other objects, calls to me. The text calls to me to perceive it, and draws me in. Most importantly, I am in relation to this object, therefore it is not outside of myself, but a part of the body. I am not in space, but I inhabit it, and explicitly do so in relations to other objects such as Carter's text. If we even consider the word "text," etymologically, it comes from the Latin word *textere*, which means, "to weave" (Camille 46). Therefore, in conjunction with the body inhabiting space, is a text not also within the world? As such, the text is interwoven within the tapestry of our being-in-the-world.

Consequently, when one considers the material body of a text, we are also considering text as a metaphorical body. For example, the way novels are structured are explicitly tied to the body. Consider the appendix, the spine, the index, the footnotes of a novel, or the novel's body on a more abstract level, like the heart of the story, or the narrator as "the voice." The text than can be considered like a speaking body. Although digressive, psychoanalysts such as Jacques Lacan posited that the unconscious is structured like language. That is, through moments of parapraxis, or slips of the tongue, one reveals unconscious thoughts. Therefore, it must be understood, that of the expansive pool of words that an individual could use when speaking, metaphorically, the words that individual chooses reveals an unconscious trauma an individual may be unaware of. For example, Carter uses the metaphor for the shadows in "The Lady of the House of Love," as those that "penetrate the woods" (109). Carter chose the metaphorical verb "penetrate" instead of seeps, flows, or runs. The conscious words that Carter chose, according to psychoanalysts, reveal the unconscious. Insofar as these words reveal unconscious thought, and particularly, trauma, than the text can also arguably be a fabric of the speaking body.

Therefore, when interacting with a text, it can be argued that we are interacting with both a metaphorical body, and also that which is objectively present within our world. If we then consider the text as a metaphorical body, than readers alter the body. In other words, readers leave slivers of bodily impression upon a text, whether it is through fingerprints, marginal notes, dog-eared bookmarking, or drops of coffee accidentally poured on its pages as one parses the text. Readers form their own palimpsests within the text through these interactions, as the writing undergoes erasure, highlighting, circling, and crossing over, in the same vein that continental philosophies postulates that our world is one embedded within being and furthermore, embedded within language, forming a palimpsest of being-in-the-world. Most importantly, these markings act like epigenetic marks that alter the expression. Through such interaction with the material body of a text, a reader alters one's access to it, and how it is later read, and understood.

We must also consider that the stories themselves are fragmented by their brief appearance within the collection, and their rapid dissolution, that is invoked by their arrival and disappearance within a single frame. These manifested slivers of discourse could simply be "turned on" or "turn off" in the same vein as epigenetic expression, and Merleau-Ponty's body image as points of access to the world, and thus, interwoven into our existence. As such, it nods towards the impact materiality has within the reader's interpretation-- as one chooses to skim through the novel, highlight a single story, or parse solely through the novel's preface. The text acts as one that moves "in and out of different tenses and time frames dissolve temporal and spatial boundaries; her narrative floats like the Marquis's castle, 'at home neither on the land nor on the water'" (Fabian 5). The altering of the text can also be thought of like the altering or adding to DNA (which, as aforementioned in Chapter 2, comprises of its own language of nucleotide bases of A, C, G, and T) that also undergo alteration and additions through methylation or acetylation. These changes or additions radically alter the transcription of information that impacts epigenetic expression, and ultimately, on a biological and physical level. Likewise, such "marks" left that either disrupt by turning "on" or allow access by turning "off" on chromatin can be compared to imprints left on texts, one that alters the way reader's access that text. Furthermore, one can trace such marks like Merleau-Ponty's case study of Schneider, the patient that lacked the synthesis of the in between realm of perception between subject and object. Most explicitly, Schneider could not "read" the composition of his own body because his access had been altered since he could not perceive or perform abstract movements.

44

Body and spatial relations can be traced in greater detail within the content of the story, and how they are informed by the theory of epigenetics. The details are: (1) the countess' environment or her home, (2) the tarot the countess reads and her somnambulism, (3) her diet, (4) the countess herself, (5) the young boy that alters the narrative, and (6) her death. Therefore, based on these threads, the rest of the thesis intends to trace how the protagonist and her environment bleed into one another, and how a change within the countess' environment reflects a change within herself.

First, it is evident within the short story that the home of the countess, or Nosferatu's daughter, informs and envelops her being. The title "The Lady of the House of Love," already reads as one embedded by the countess' ancestors, as she is a vampire queen that inhabits or by extension is the "house of love." The house is a foil to the countess aesthetically, as her home is described as a castle rotting away beneath the countess' feet. The windows are barred shut, with distressed red clothes strewn throughout the house either as wallpaper or furnishing, and stained with "ominous marks like those left on the sheets by dead lovers" (Carter 108). Unlike the dying home, she is a vampire and is cursed with immortality of her ancestors. Yet, despite this foil, it is what lies within the house that I would like to highlight, and what I argue, extends into her being. The house is comprised of ghostly occupants that haunt every corner of the home as shadows. When she walks through the halls and "through the galleries where the painted eyes of family portraits briefly flickered as they passed," and where "all the roses her dead mother planted have grown up into a huge, spiked wall that incarcerates her in the castle of her inheritance" (110). Simply, the countess has not only inherited a space, and a familial curse, but her ancestors themselves that still loom, and still dilate in her

being. These inhabitants inform her environment, which in turn, bleed into her own

corporeal existence. The environment continues to bleed, hypothetically ad infinitum,

until it is eventually altered. Until then, the countess is considered as a closed circuit of

repetition that repeatedly sings the same song. Yet, there are a few notable details that

must be unpacked in order to understand how the circuit ruptures.

Unlike what was posited in the introduction, where critics often tout Carter as a

feminist that radically reverse gender roles, and breaks subject/object conventions using

mirrors, "The Lady of the House of Love," does not use these conventions. The

conventions of a mirror are not used because the protagonist is a vampire queen, and

although the mirrors do exist within the home, they do not reflect. The mirrors are

illustrated by the "cracked mirror suspended from a wall does not reflect a presence" or

when the servant is asked to "to keep mirrors and all reflective surfaces away from her"

(Carter 107, 110). Instead, Carter uses echoing[23] for the protagonist to, in a way, view

herself as both subject and object because she views herself in relation to her home, and

to the young man when he later enters the castle. Vampires are traditionally associated

---

[23] Derrida address the myth of Narcissus and Echo in the film *Derrida*. In Greek mythology, Echo is cursed by jealous gods to never speak, and instead, can only repeat the words of others. Narcissus, on the other hand, falls in love within his own image as he stared into a pool of water, and dies of a love lost. Echo falls in love with Narcissus, and communicates with him by cleverly re-appropriating his last syllables, thus making them her own, and no longer just repetitions. Derrida concludes that both are blind. Echo is blind in her speech, and Narcissus blind in that he only views himself as subject within the mirror, unlike the protagonists that view themselves in relation to other objects in Carter's tales.

with creatures of the night such as bats. These animals rely on echolocation in order to be mobile within a space, thus only using objects within that space to orient itself and navigate the world. Considering that such motility indicates an envelopment of the body being the world, the countess is also strictly viewing herself in relations to objects around her. In the short story, the narrator states that the countess "is herself a cave full of echoes, she is a system of repetitions, she is a closed circuit" and furthermore, that "her voice is filled with distant sonorities, like reverberations in a cave" (Carter 108). As such, the echoing is not only indicative of how the countess views herself, and her own space and body, but also her use of language.

As an individual composed like a mirror, consisting of reverberation and echoes, such instances also signify moments of fragmentation. Although she is illustrated as enclosed and far removed, echoes within a circuit force the protagonist to face herself, and defer[24] "definition." For example, when we consider fragmentation, a text or novel is comprised of words, or fragments. Furthermore, in light of deconstruction, such words or fragments postpone meaning by an endless chain of signifiers. That is, if we look at the word echo within the dictionary, in the search for meaning of echo are other words. And if one were to research the definitions of those words, they would also defer to more definitions that are comprised of more words, and those words need further definition. Therefore, through such deferrals of meaning, the chain of signification is endless. Words, like the protagonist, are a circuit of echoes. When we even consider epigenetics,

---

[24] See Crunelle-Vanrigh on binary opposition and différence in Angela Carter's "The Courtship of Mr.Lyon"

case studies such as the Dutch Hunger winter show how genome expressions are actually deferred from an individual's ancestors. The reason why she sings the same tune is because she is an extension of that cave which is her home, and the deferment of genetic vampirism. Further, the "text" that is comprised of echoes within her home weaves into the countess' body. For example, the echo of her ancestors embeds her biological being, as she is informed by this text, like the base pairs that inform her vampire DNA. Pushing the theme of différance a bit further, the novel itself follows this theme of echoing. Each short story within the collection defers to the other. They all contain the same plot, yet have radically different shells that continue or defers their central meaning: tales of women subverting patriarchal figures. For example, the first short story "The Bloody Chamber," reinvents Charles Perrault's tale of Bluebeard, where the female protagonist is victorious against the sadistic and murderous Marquis. The following short story, "The Courtship of Mr. Lyon," leaves the reader with the distinct taste of deja vu, as it portrays a young woman struggling against being treated as object by male patriarchal figures in a reinvention of the beauty and the beast. Although the methods of subversion are distinct within each tale, the overarching plot is still deferred from one tale to the next, until the final story "Wolf Alice." It is as if the same protagonist struggles with a similar patriarchal figure infinitely, yet under the veil of a different tale. Explicitly, in the "The Lady of the House of Love," the countess struggles against the single patriarch within the tale: her home or her environment that is generated from her male ancestor Vlad the Impaler. The reader understands the countess' struggle in her continuous casting of her tarot deck that act like slivers of resistance. Such an act echoes with hope that one day the cards may change.

Whether the countess casts her tarot out of habit, or out of hope, it is revealed that these cards have been used at such great lengths that the image on the surface of the cards have disappeared with use. As a textual material object, the cards have undergone erasure. Yet the Countess can still read the traces left behind from the image that once was. Furthermore, the countess reads the same tarot: "In her dream, she would like to be human; but she does not know if that is possible. The Tarot always shows the same configuration: always she turns up La Papesse, La Mort, La Tour Abolie" (Carter 105). The unwavering tarot acts like the horizon of possibility that the body anticipates. Although the tarot reads the same outcome in relations to her environment and perception, it is still open to possibilities. Furthermore, like the intentional arc, knowledge allows an individual to act in according to one's environment by binding[25] the body to the world. Yet, the intentional arc also consider the past in terms of what was, and future in terms of what could be, like the countess' tarot.

The short story also portrays the countess as a somnambulist. The narrator states, the "somnambulist helplessly perpetuates her ancestral crimes" (Carter, 107). Further, Carter writes that the castle "surrounds her habitual tormented somnambulism, her life or imitation of life" (110). A somnambulist is simply an individual who walks in their sleep. When an individual sleepwalks, they perform normal activities within their homes as if they were awake. As such, when an individual is a somnambulist, they are also performing movements based on mental mapping. When considering somnambulist's

---

[25] Boundaries do not only separate, but also *bind* one to the other. Horizons, such as the horizons described by Heidegger, are also boundaries that both divide and separate.

49

mental mapping, Merleau-Ponty's synthesis of primary and secondary meaning comes to mind. Through primary meaning, the world just exists; for example, the primary meaning of my bedroom is just the blueprint of my room, and the objects it holds. Secondary meaning is then obtained through my motility within that space (referring back to echoing, and echolocation in relation to objects). Because I understand the primary meaning of my bedroom, I can than walk around that space with my eyes closed. The synthesis, as seen by the countess who walks throughout her home with eyes closed in her somnambulism, is the world structure where her body incorporates space and time.

Another element that needs to be considered in the study of the countess and her epigenetic expression, and consequently, her body and spatial relations, is her diet. As a vampire countess, her diet consists of consuming the blood of young men. As a child, the blood she would consume was primarily derived from animals, yet even then, the countess abhorred the food that she needed to consume to survive. When the countess ate rabbits, she would entertain taking them home, and feeding them beds of lettuce. As she began consuming the blood of young men, she is described as having "cheeks mixed with tears; her keeper probes her fingernails for her with a little silver toothpick to get rid of the fragments of skin and bone that have lodged there" (Carter, 111). Therefore, such imagery elucidates that the countess was disgusted by the cruelty of her diet, and longed to consume meals that comprise of vegetables and grains. Yet, her physiological and phenotypical traits were suited for her diet, as she is described as having fingernails and teeth shaped like spikes of destiny, and "sharpened on centuries of corpses" (111). It is crucial to understand that expressions alter from both a change of environment and a

50

change in diet. As aforementioned in the epigenetics chapter, diet is also a stressor that can impact epigenetic expression, as observed in the case studies of the Dutch Famine, or even the consumption of royal jelly by queen honeybees. Consider how the countess' diet was solely based on blood, and that her environment was also just as consistent, since it was a space that was literally embedded by her ancestors as her own flesh is coupled with her diet, and the environment. In tandem with Merleau-Ponty, and the theory of epigenetics, she is a product of her environment, since it both informs and sustains her. The countess' ancestral inheritance and body and spatial relations are self-evident, as she "sprang from the loins of Vlad the Impaler who picnicked on corpses in the forests of Transylvania" (Carter 111).

Finally, the countess herself even dresses according to her environment, dawning her mother's wedding dress[26] everyday. The dress has transformed with age into a consumed grey gown that hangs off the pale and effulgent countess. The narrator describes her as a creature of distinct beauty, where her features cry with deformity, as she lacked the "touching imperfections that reconcile us to the imperfection of the human condition. Her beauty is the symptom of her disorder, of her soullessness" (114). Such revulsion to imperfection is a common term in art and film called the uncanny valley. She is perfect to such an extent that it is uncanny to those that perceive her, and as such, viewers respond to her in disgust due to the jarring lack of humanity within her beauty. As aforementioned, she is an "imitation of life." Thus, she acts like a tableau of mimetic art perfected. Furthermore, she radiates the beauty inherited by her ancestors, and is

---

[26] see Henke, page 56

"herself is a haunted house. She does not possess herself; her ancestors sometimes come and peer out of the windows of her eyes and that is very frightening" (Carter 113). Here, the connection between the countess and her environment is clear, and further codified by the ghosts that peer from her eyes, like ghosts that peer out of windows.

She is the bird that sings the same song as her ancestors and she is the " hereditary commandant of the army of shadows" (Carter 115). That is until a change in her environment, and likewise a change in her diet, alters this expression. The alteration occurs through the young virginal boy that enters the castle. The young man is highlighted as a "being, rooted in change and time, is about to collide with the timeless Gothic eternity of the vampires, all for whom all is as it always has been and will be, whose cards always fall in the same pattern" (112). It is the arrival of the young boy, where she is not only altered, as is her environment, but it radically also alters her horizon. For example, as the young man enters the castle the tarot cards read differently. Instead of reading wisdom, death, and dissolution, the tarot instead reads both love and death. The echo of repetitions becomes ruptured, and she can sing a new song. Provided that she was a system of echoes, the new song harkens to the patients that suffered from the phenomenon of a phantom limb as highlighted by Merleau-Ponty. These patients had to restructure their perception in order to "turn off" the experience of the phenomenon, and likewise, the countess restructures her perception when the young man arrives. Restructuring can also be considered in light of the mature frog nucleus that was implanted into the unfertilized egg. As the environment changes, the frog nucleus will reset or restructure itself according to the environment. Therefore, the protagonist is a system of repetitions until a disruption occurs within her environment, and thus shatters and restructures this cave. The change in her environment begins with the boy entering the castle. The boy's entrance already her shifts the tarot or horizon, until he ultimately kissing her hand when she wounds herself, and lovingly cares after her. For example, he "gently takes her hand away from her, and dabs the blood with his own handkerchief, but still it spurts out. And so he put his mouth to the wound. He will kiss it better for her" (Carter 123). Through his arrival within her environment, she denies drinking his blood, and being further wielded by her ancestors. In that moment, "the mechanism within her fails her" and as such, her epigenetic expression alters and she is no longer a vampire (Carter 122). Simply put, her previous expression that derived from her old environment "turned off," to match the new environment she was in. Let us recall monozygotic twins, and although they shared the same genetic makeup, different environments had "marked" them to have radically different genetic expressions. Therefore, as the countess transform from vampire to human, through both an altered environment and a change in diet, it is not farfetched to connect such changes to a radical change in epigenetic expression. Although dramatized, such fiction nods towards changes in our genetic makeup that occurs by environmental stressors, and are very much, a part of our biological makeup. Further, if we are to understand this change in light of Merleau-Ponty's philosophy, the countess restructured her perception of the world as the world had altered her access. She has consumed a new world, and as such, embodies it. It is not that the outside determines her, but that "nothing determines me from outside, not because nothing acts upon me, but, on the contrary, because I am from the start outside myself and open to the world" (Merleau-Ponty 292). Finally, due to her transformation, the countess then dies. As such,

53

in transformation, she is also being-towards-death. It is in death that "she looks far older, less beautiful and so, for the first time fully human" (Carter 124). Therefore, the countess is an embodiment of her home, and as the home is altered the countess also undergoes alteration.

As such, it is evident that the disciplines of science, philosophy, and literature are also embedded within the text, and alter one another. Such conversations are not only important to highlight, but to divulge and participate in. The following concluding chapter will stress that such conversations need further discussion based on the claims and evidence posited in this chapter.

CONCLUDING THOUGHTS:

"There was a house we all had in common and it was called the past, even though we'd
lived in different rooms." –Angela Carter, Wise Children

Let us consider this thesis as an object, and as such, one that reflects my
environment, and thus, is also reflecting within your very own space. As an object within
your space, and in keeping with the aforementioned theories where the environment (and
the objects within it) weave into being, I apologize for such an intimate intrusion of
privacy. Jokes aside, since this thesis is one that both has explicated and performed these
theories, while providing bridges for both body and space, and the disciplines of science,
literature, and continental philosophy, it would only be fair to afford the reader a sliver of
insight on how this object came to "be". The idea for this thesis is indebted to a
conversation I had with my father one night. The two of us often view our passions on
opposite ends of the spectrum, as my father is an entomologist who would coax me as a
young girl to pin insects onto Styrofoam cushions on days such as Take Your Child to
Work Day. In contrast, I always had an affinity for the arts. As such, our conversations
were usually informative, one detailing their studies to the other, until our conversations
were altered by a study we had both encountered on epigenetics. We then were able to
thread these ideas into both disciplines, and found that what we once believed were
radically separate, unlike the body and its environment, were deeply intertwined. And
this is what this thesis aimed to be--- an intertwining of ideas that I argue not only already
occur, but are also necessary to pursue.

That is, ideas should act within collaboration, subverting hierarchal positioning
seen in several binaries such as subject/object, body/space, man/woman, science/art, and

etc. We see such positioning in our school systems, where the abundance of funding is funneled into STEM fields (science + technology + engineering + math). According to *The New York Times,* "several Republicans have portrayed a liberal arts education as an expendable, sometimes frivolous luxury that taxpayers should not be expected to pay for." (Cohen) Further, the University of Kentucky has already proposed cuts in the humanities, in order to form incentive programs for students in STEM disciplines that are both "intellectually and professionally rewarding." On March 23rd, 2015, on the U.S. Department of Education website, President Barack Obama stressed the importance of STEM fields, stating that: "Science is more than a school subject, or the periodic table, or the properties of waves. It is an approach to the world, a critical way to understand and explore and engage with the world, and then have the capacity to change that world…" Yet, has this thesis not accomplished all of the above, both exploring and engaging with the world as an extension of body, and vice versa? And has it not done so with further success by combining the disciplines of science, literature, and continental philosophy, acting within a spectrum of ideas? Conversations such as these cannot be ignored, as they are already naturally occurring, like the threads this thesis has traced within Angela Carter's "The Lady of the House of Love." Like the world, that like the phantom limb, calls to be read, to be moved, and to be lived in, and like the body that calls to be altered by the world, this thesis calls for change (changes like those occurring in the shift in frameworks from STEM to STEAM (science + technology + engineering + arts + math) proposed by education programs such as The Rhode Island School of Design). As Albert Einstein stated in his interview with George Viereck in the *Saturday Evening Post* on the 26th of October in 1929: "I am enough of an artist to draw freely upon my imagination.

Imagination is more important than knowledge. Knowledge is limited. Imagination encircles the world" (17). To conclude, let us draw freely inside, and outside of these disciplines, as the boundaries we place do not only separate these fields, but also binds one with other, and as such, are worth pursuing.

REFERENCES

Allis, C. David, Thomas Jenuwein, and Danny Reinberg, eds. *Epigenetics*. Cold Spring Harbor, NY: Cold Spring Harbor Laboratory, 2007. Print.

Barker, Paul. "The Return of the Magic Storyteller." *The Independent*. Independent Digital News and Media, 07 Jan. 1995. Web. 02 Feb. 2016.

Barthes, Roland. "Death of the Author." *Image, Music, Text*. Trans. Stephen Heath. New York: and Wang, 1977. Print.

Camille, Michael. "Sensations of the Page: Imaging Technologies and Medieval Illuminated Manuscripts." *The Iconic Page in Manuscript, Print and Digital Culture*. University of Michigan Press, 1998. Print.

Caputo, John. *Deconstruction in a Nutshell*. Fordham University Press New York, 1997. Print.

Carey, Nessa. *The Epigenetics Revolution.* New York: Columbia University Press, 2013. Print.
Carter, Angela. *The Bloody Chamber*. Vintage Books, 2006. Print

---. *The Sadeian Woman and the Ideology of Pornography.* Vintage Books, 2007. Print.

Cohen, Patricia. "A Rising Call to Promote STEM Education and Cut Liberal Arts Funding." *The New York Times*. The New York Times, 21 Feb. 2016. Web. 23 Feb. 2016.

Crunelle-vanrigh, Anny. "The Logic of the Same and Différance: "the Courtship of Mr Lyon"". *Marvels & Tales* 12.1 (1998): 116–132. JSTOR.

Derrida. Dir. Kirby Dick and Amy Kofman. Zeitgeist Films, 2002. Film.

deSade, Marquis. *Juliette*. Grove Press, 1994. Print.

--.*Justine, or the Misfortunes of Virtue*. Oxford University Press, 2013. Print.

Diprose, Rosalyn, and Reynolds, Jack. *Merleau-Ponty Key Concepts.* Stocksfield Hall: Acumen Publishing Limited, 2008. Print.

Fabian, Jenny. "Angela Carter's Interrogation of Authority in *The Bloody Chamber*." *The London Grip*. N.p., 2010. Web. 02 Feb. 2016.

Felsenfeld, Gary. "The Evolution of Epigenetics." Perspectives in Biology and Medicine 57.1 (2014) JSTOR.

Hass, Lawrence. *Merleau-Ponty's Philosophy.* Bloomington: Indiana University Press, 2008. Print.

Henke, Suzette A. "A Bloody Shame: Angela Carter's Shameless Postmodern Fairy Tales". *The Female Face of Shame.* Ed. ERICA L. JOHNSON and PATRICIA MORAN. Indiana University Press, 2013. 48–60. JSTOR.

Hodara, Susan. "Putting the A in STEAM." *The New York Times.* The New York Times, 26 July 2014. Web. 23 Feb. 2016.

Keats, John. *Complete Poems and Selected Letters of John Keats.* New York: Modern Library, 2001. Print.

King, Magda, and John Llewellyn. *A Guide to Heidegger's Being and Time.* Albany: State U of New York, 2001. Print.

Kearney, Richard. *Modern Movements in European Philosophy.* Manchester: Manchester University Press, 1987. Print.

Matthews, Eric. *Merleau-Ponty a Guide for the Perplexed.* London: Continuum International Pub. Group, 2006. Print.

Merleau-Ponty, Maurice. *The Structure of Behavior.* Trans. Alden L. Fisher. Boston: Beacon, 1963. Print.

---. *Phenomenology of Perception.* Trans. Donald A. Landes. New York: Routledge, 2012. Print.

Moore, David. *The Developing Genome: An Introduction to Behavioral Epigenetics.* New York: Oxford, 2015. Print.

Rock, Irvin, and Palmer, Stephen "The Legacy of Gestalt Psychology." *Scientific American.* 263.6 (1990) Web.

Sauer, Brooke. *Histones...What Are Those?* Web. 22 Feb. 2016.

Schanoes, Veronica L. "Book as Mirror, Mirror as Book: The Significance of the Looking-glass in Contemporary Revisions of Fairy Tales". *Journal of the Fantastic in the Arts* 20.1 (75) (2009): 5–23. JSTOR.

Schwegel, John. *DNA Double Helix.* Digital image. *The Atlantic.* 29 Nov. 2012. Web.

Steeves, James B. *Imagining Bodies.* Pittsburgh: Duquesene University Press, 2004. Print.

Vierick, George. "What Life Means to Einstein." *The Saturday Evening Post. 26 October, 1929. Web. 23 Feb, 2016.*

Weinhold, Bob. "Epigenetics: The Science of Change." Environmental Health Perspectives 114.3 (2006) JSTOR.

Ingram Content Group UK Ltd.
Milton Keynes UK
UKHW020639050623
422889UK00016B/1978